A DANCE LESSON
BY DAVID WILTSE

★

DRAMATISTS
PLAY SERVICE
INC.

A DANCE LESSON received a workshop production at the Long Wharf Theatre (Arvin Brown, Artistic Director; M. Edgar Rosenblum, Executive Director) in New Haven, Connecticut, opening on March 7, 1989. It was directed by Gordon Edelstein; the set design was by Hugh Landwehr; the lighting design was by Steven Rust; the sound design was by Brent Paul Evans; the costume design was by Jean Routt and Melinda Watt; and the production stage manager was Ruth M. Feldman. The cast was as follows:

DAN HAUSER .... Tracy Griswold
SUSAN HAUSER .... Susan Pellegrino
JAY HAUSER .... Josh Charles
JACK STONE .... Ben Siegler
SMITTY .... Rob Harris Kramer
JASON .... Eric Conger

A DANCE LESSON received its world premiere at the Long Wharf Theatre (Arvin Brown, Artistic Director; M. Edgar Rosenblum, Executive Director) in New Haven, Connecticut, opening on October 27, 1989. It was directed by Gordon Edelstein; the set design was by Hugh Landwehr; the lighting design was by Pat Collins; the costume design was by David Murin; and the production stage manager was Ruth M. Feldman. The cast was as follows:

DAN HAUSER .... John Cunningham
SUSAN HAUSER .... Debra Mooney
JAY HAUSER .... Josh Charles
JACK STONE .... Quentin O'Brien
SMITTY .... Rob Kramer
JASON .... Eric Conger

CHARACTERS

HAUSER, a strong, moral man. Good-humored, salt of the earth. Midwestern.

SUSAN, his wife, attractive, intelligent, less serious, also Midwestern.

JACK STONE, charming, confident, attractive, athletic, about 30.

JAY, son of Hauser and Susan, 16.

SMITTY, Jay's buddy, also 16, less assertive than Jay, shy.

JASON, Jay as an adult, now Hauser's age. Serious but with an affectionate side and a sense of humor.

PLACE

The living room/dining room of a middle-class Midwestern family.

TIME

The recent past.

A DANCE LESSON

ACT ONE

The living room/dining room of a middle-class Midwestern family of the recent past. At rise, the set is dark or behind a scrim. Jason enters and stands in front of the set.

JASON. Let me tell you a story that haunts me. I've tried to drive it from my memory a number of ways, but it won't go; and I've tried to change it by wrapping it in the easy sentiment of nostalgia, the way an oyster makes a pearl from an irritating grain of sand — but it won't change. It is what it is ... and it won't leave me until I can accept it. *(Lights up on set. Jason steps onto set, touches furniture, wonders at the past. With a rueful nostalgia, as if he can't quite believe it.)* This was my world. I was formed and shaped here, within this house and the town beyond it, shaped in ways I didn't realize then and am startled to discover even now. The town is Cascade, Nebraska, the heart of the heart of the nation. It is a small town, it makes the newspapers only if a grain elevator explodes. Otherwise, nothing of significance to anyone else happens here except the forging of the American soul. The time is the past, when everyone was younger. We were mean to people and open about it, convinced of our right to be mean ... Everyone I loved is in this story, which carries the bitter message that love alone is not enough. The facts may not be right, but the story is true, or partly true, or true enough ... *(Enter Daniel Hauser, singing, with good feeling. He is tying his tie, getting ready for the new day.)*
HAUSER. *(Singing.)* "Bringing in the sheaves, bringing in the sheaves, we shall come rejoicing, bringing in the sheaves!"
JASON. *(Brightening.)* He was always so cheerful in the mornings. He would roll out of bed with a song on his lips. It used to drive my mother crazy.

HAUSER. *(Calling cheerfully.)* Rise and shine, Jay! Up and at 'em! *(Hauser sits at the dining room table, sips coffee that is waiting there, glances at some papers from his briefcase ... Enter Susan Hauser, Daniel's wife, carrying a bowl of breakfast cereal for Hauser. She is still tired. She is dressed in a dowdy housecoat. To greet her, gaily.)* "When the frost is on the pumpkin and the fodder's in the shock, and you hear the kyouck and gobble of the struttin' turkey-cock ... " *(Susan recoils at the cheerfulness as if hit by a wave, then recovers and serves him. Singing.)* "Oh, it's them's the times a feller is a-feelin' at his best ... "

HAUSER and JASON. *(Simultaneously.)* "With the risin' sun to greet him from a night of peaceful rest ... " *(Susan draws a worn smile and nods patiently. Hauser declaims this poem with an exaggerated hayseed quality, at once both liking the poem yet being aware of its corniness.)*

JASON. *(Continues.)* He seemed to live in an eternal Thanksgiving in his mind, all rosy cheeks and frosted pumpkins. Or so I remember it. He couldn't have, really. He was as old as I am now. And he was the county attorney, he prosecuted the drunk drivers, the petty thieves, farmers who turned their shotguns on their neighbors ... He saw the dregs — and yet such optimism.

HAUSER. *(Calling.)* Jay! Rise and shine! *(To Susan.)* And what's on your agenda for the day, my dear?

SUSAN. *(Tentatively.)* I'm going to do the laundry, then I thought I might stop by the radio station.

HAUSER. Oh?

SUSAN. Mr. Goldberg is going to be there today, and he wants to discuss my ideas for the program.

HAUSER. I thought we decided you weren't going to do a program.

SUSAN. I thought we said we'd think about it ... It would only be fifteen minutes a week, Dan. I'm sure I could do it.

HAUSER. Oh, I'm sure you could, too. The question is whether you should.

JASON. It was a radio interview show and she had already done a prototype, chatting with a local banker who had just come back from a trip to Egypt. My father and I listened with acute embarrassment. Not that she was bad — just that she was ours. My discomfort was mixed with pride, but my father's was more complex. No man then wanted anyone to think his wife *had* to work. And there was a certain mocking tone to his remarks that seemed to cover a genuine concern that this bit of celebrity might have caused her star to shine brighter than his own. It breached their agreement, it changed their relationship, one in which he was very comfortable. What bothered him most was my mother's respectful, deferential, passive refusal to give it up. He was not quite prepared to "put his foot down" on the issue, and she was not about to give it up for anything else. They tugged at it on the edges, like sleepers vying for control of the covers. Neither would admit that a contest was joined.

SUSAN. I don't think it will do any lasting harm for me to meet with Mr. Goldberg.

HAUSER. He's sharp, Susan. Don't expect to come away with everything you had going in. Our Mr. Goldberg sets a price upon things.

SUSAN. He seems a very nice little man.

HAUSER. We had a meeting with him at the Chamber of Commerce. He was pushing for some concessions, of course.

SUSAN. He's allowed to make a living.

HAUSER. Of course he's entitled to every advantage within the law. And he'll take it, too.

JASON. They were shaped as I was, no more to blame.

SUSAN. *(Casually.)* Oh, and Jack said he might drop over this afternoon.

HAUSER. Good thing we're next door. He'd be hard-pressed for entertainment without you.

SUSAN. You don't object, do you?

HAUSER. Don't be silly. I like Jack.

SUSAN. I'm sure we all like Jack. And Daniel ... I think it's time you had a talk with Jay.

HAUSER. What's he up to now?

SUSAN. Well ... it's his sheets.

HAUSER. What about his sheets?

SUSAN. ... they're soiled every morning.

HAUSER. Ah.

SUSAN. Yes, ah.

HAUSER. Nothing you can do about a boy's dreams, sweetheart. It's just nature and a teenager's imagination. Everyone's bound to have an accident now and then at that age.

SUSAN. These are not dreams.

HAUSER. How do you know?

SUSAN. His pajamas aren't soiled.

HAUSER. I see ... Well, youth.

SUSAN. That's all right for you to say, but I have to wash the sheets.

HAUSER. Have you talked to him about it?

SUSAN. Me? That's your place, don't you think? I'm his mother.

HAUSER. You want *me* to talk to him about it?

SUSAN. I know it's embarrassing, but I think you have to do it.

HAUSER. It's not a question of embarrassment, it's just — a gentle word from his mother ...

SUSAN. Daniel, I don't know anything about it. It's your place.

HAUSER. JAY! Come down here!

SUSAN. Don't be mean.

HAUSER. Am I ever mean to the boy?

SUSAN. Not mean, Dan. Sometimes you're a little gruff.

HAUSER. I'm not gruff.

SUSAN. Sometimes you're a little short with him. He's only a boy.

HAUSER. He's sixteen. When I was a boy ...

JASON. Oh, that phrase. "When I was a boy ... " It summoned up the golden age of Pericles. Times were hard. Men labored long, lived clean, hewed to a code of ethics sadly tarnished today. And all things were possible to a lad whose heart was pure. My heart, of course, was never pure. Innocent, perhaps, but as soiled as my sheets. *(Jay enters, a boy of sixteen, disheveled and tired.)* My God, what a lout. Tuck your shirt in.

SUSAN. Good morning, Lambie.

JAY. *(Grunting.)* Morning.

HAUSER. I think we can do a little better by your mother than that, don't you?

JAY. *(False brightness.)* Good morning, Mother dear.

HAUSER. Tuck your shirt in.

JAY. This is the way everybody wears them, Dad.

HAUSER. If everybody jumped off the roof, would you do that, too?

JASON. It was always the same example. Was there ever a time when people jumped off the roof en masse?

SUSAN. Eat your breakfast, Lambie.

HAUSER. Your mother is meeting with Mr. Goldberg, that little man who owns the radio station.

JASON. Always that "little" man.

HAUSER. She's on her way to stardom, eh? *(Hauser winks and chuckles, trying to enlist Jay's support. Jay obliges by chuckling too. Susan exits, hurt.)* Only teasing, Sue! ... What's on your agenda for the day?

JAY. School.

HAUSER. When I was a boy, I was always eager to get to school.

There's nothing so exciting as the opportunity to *learn*.

JAY. You probably didn't have to study the Constitution in Social Science.

HAUSER. Let me tell you a remarkable thing they won't teach you about the Constitution. That document is the first time in history that the ruling class of people set limits on itself without being forced to. Those men, who could have said whatever they wanted to, said *it is the law* that we will tolerate others who aren't like us. They made tolerance a law! Isn't that something?

JAY. Yeah.

HAUSER. See, Jay, they were all human. They knew they had their failings and they didn't trust themselves to always be fair and just on their own. So the ruling majority *ceded rights* to the minority. They had their prejudices but would not give in to them. It's a miracle of intellectual fairness over emotion.

JAY. Yeah.

HAUSER. Do you see what I'm getting at, Jay?

JAY. It's a miracle.

JASON. He's trying to teach you something! Why are you so afraid of learning? Take advantage of it!

HAUSER. They said, "We will act morally, whether we want to or not!" And we do!

JASON. *(Sadly.)* We don't, Dad.

HAUSER. Order tempered by compassion, that's our system. It's a good way to run your life, too.

JASON. Compassion.

HAUSER. Well, end of sermon, but it doesn't do any harm to think about it.

JAY. *(Flip.)* Okay, I'll think about it. *(Hauser fixes him with a stare. Jay grows uneasy, realizes he has overstepped.)* I mean I will, I'll think about it.

HAUSER. Okay, Jay … Jay … So, is there anything you want to tell me?

JAY. About what?

JASON. Instant freewheeling guilt. What have I been caught at now?

HAUSER. About your nocturnal activities.

JAY. I don't know what you mean.

HAUSER. Your mother tells me your sheets are soiled.

JAY. What?!

JASON. To die, just give me a chance to die before the conversation goes any further.

JAY. No, they're not!

HAUSER. That's making a lot of unnecessary work for your mother.

JAY. No, it's not.

HAUSER. I don't imagine she's making up a story, is she?

JAY. I'm sure not doing it!

HAUSER. Jay ... *(Gestures for Jay to sit down.)* I believe a priest would tell you it's a sin, but since we're not Catholic, I don't know what that has to do with it. The point is, sometimes everybody has the temptation.

JAY. Not me.

HAUSER. Jay, *everybody* has the temptation at your age.

JAY. Even you? *(Pause.)*

HAUSER. I was your age once, too.

JAY. *You* did it?

HAUSER. I didn't say I did it, son. I said I was your age once. I practiced self-discipline.

JAY. So do I, Dad.

HAUSER. Jay, we are what we make of ourselves. Knowing the right thing to do is seldom the problem, but choosing the right thing can be difficult. I could be a very different person than I am if I let myself, but I have willed myself to choose the right things in life. You are what you make of yourself. Well, a word to the wise, Jay, that's all I'm saying. Your mother works hard enough as it is ... *(Hauser starts toward the kitchen, then turns back, with some difficulty.)* ... Self-discipline isn't infallible. Try the bathroom. *(Jay is amazed at this semi-admission.)*

JASON. That constituted sex education. Of course, I'd tried the bathroom. And the closets, and the kitchen, and the garage, and behind the hedge, and once, for erotic reasons that now escape me, *under* the bed. *(Hauser and Susan enter from the kitchen.)*

HAUSER. Don't slouch, Jay. Throw your shoulders back.

SUSAN. Good luck in court.

HAUSER. It won't be luck, sweetheart. They're guilty.

SUSAN. Who's the judge?

HAUSER. Lurtsema.

SUSAN. *(Indignantly.)* That man is an illiterate Bohunk.

HAUSER. *(To Jay.)* That means he opposed your mother on the library expansion.

SUSAN. Well, I'm sorry, but he is. He's never treated you the way he should, Dan, and you know it.

HAUSER. He's never treated me the way he should — but he's treated me according to the law. *(Wink to Jay.)* I'll have to wait for the coronation.

SUSAN. I'm surprised he can even read the law.

HAUSER. He doesn't very well. Fortunately I'm there to interpret it for him.

JAY. Is this that burglar?

HAUSER. That was last week. He's on his way to Lincoln now.

JAY. What's the case, Dad?

HAUSER. *(Slight pause.)* Sodomy.

JAY. Somebody did it with animals?

HAUSER. *(Sternly.)* Not with animals.

JAY. Then what?

JASON. Don't sound so eager. A boy from high school was rumored to have had his way with a calf on the family farm — a possibility the rest of us viewed with mixed horror and curiosity. At least it was a fellow mammal. That put him way ahead of the rest of us.

HAUSER. Jay, would you please finish cleaning out the garage this afternoon. I want it hosed down in there.

JAY. Ah, Dad, come on …

HAUSER. What was that? Want to make something of it? Elevate thy dukes.

JAY. Alright … *(Hauser strikes a John L. Sullivan pose. Jay squares off in modern boxing pose. This is a time-honored ritual for them. Jay bounces and tries to slip in a punch into Hauser's midsection.)*

HAUSER. The "egg beater." *(Hauser twirls his arms in front of himself like an egg beater. Jay cannot penetrate.)* Impenetrable … *(He stops.)* The garage. *(Jay stops boxing, nods resignedly. Hauser grins and immediately turns to Susan with a wink.)* Still too fast for him. Goodbye, sweetheart. *(Hauser kisses Susan on the cheek.)*

SUSAN. How does my hair look, Dan?

HAUSER. Fine. See you at dinner. Have a good day, Speedo. *(Jay hands Hauser briefcase.)*

JAY. You, too, Dad. *(Hauser exits.)*

JASON. Off he would go to do moral battle, every day of his life. And we so proud we could burst. If our parents help us define ourselves, he showed me very clearly who I was and would become. We were safe in his shadow, sheltered there like saplings under a giant oak.

JAY. What's sodomy?

SUSAN. I don't know. Do I look just horrible?

JAY. You look great.

SUSAN. No, I mean it, Jay. I hate my hair.

JAY. Your hair looks great, Mom. The dictionary just says "certain unnatural acts."

SUSAN. *(Annoyed.)* Then that's what it means. Now hurry up or you'll be late for school, Lambie.

JAY. Don't call me Lambie.

SUSAN. Go on to school. Aren't you supposed to invite Katie Reed to the junior prom today?

JAY. I'm not *supposed* to. I was just thinking about it. I'm not sure I even want to go to the prom.

SUSAN. Now, Jay.

JAY. I mean it. It's just a dance.

SUSAN. You're going to have to start dating sometime, honey.

JAY. I'm going to! I'm going to! God!

SUSAN. Go on to school now. *(Susan exits into kitchen. Jay slouches off.)*

JASON. Throw your shoulders back! What a lout ... My mother was infatuated. His name was Jack Stone. His elderly parents lived next door to us, but he had left town ten years ago after graduating from high school. Now, suddenly, he was back, living with his parents for what was understood to be a temporary stay "until he got on his feet again." Just what knocked him off his feet, no one knew for certain. Some said a nervous breakdown, which seemed hardly credible in someone so robust and cheerful. My mother's theory was that he was recovering from some tragic, *Camille*-like love affair. I think she particularly liked the idea because Camille was an older woman. I preferred to think he was hiding out after some dangerous — but dishonorable — brush with the law. Piracy, for instance. *(Susan enters from kitchen. She is now dressed more smartly than before. She preens quickly, excitedly, before a mirror.)* Whatever his true story, he had inflamed in my mother that fiery itch of the imagination we call love. *(Jack Stone enters, a pleasant, virile man of thirty.)*

SUSAN. Oh, Jack. I was expecting you, I must look a mess.

JACK. You look sensational.

SUSAN. No, really, my hair looks awful, don't you think?

JACK. I like it. It sets your face off just right.

SUSAN. Do you really? I wasn't sure I liked it ...

JACK. I don't know how Mr. Hauser keeps his hands off you.

(Jack gives Susan a flower which he has kept behind his back.)

SUSAN. Jack, how sweet.

JACK. I found it growing next to Bletcher's cornfield at the edge of town. It looked so lonely. I thought I'd bring it to someone just as pretty.

SUSAN. Oh Jack, look what I look like. What were you doing at Bletcher's field?

JACK. I went to watch the corn grow, couldn't find anything more exciting to do.

SUSAN. I know. Do you want some coffee? ... It's millet, by the way.

JACK. What is?

SUSAN. Bletcher grows millet, not corn. Or at least that's what Daniel tells me. Not that I asked. They look alike to me.

JACK. God, Susan, how do you stand it here? I mean, it's all right for some of them, but you're not like that, you're bright, you're sensitive, you have a good sense of humor ...

SUSAN. Well, go *on*.

JACK. You know what I mean.

SUSAN. Yes, but I like to *hear* it.

JACK. You must hear it everyday. Just step onto the street and the locals call out "There's Susan Hauser, creature extraordinaire."

SUSAN. "Extraordinaire" is not in the local vocabulary. They're more apt to say, "There goes Susan Hauser, she's taking on airs." It's like living in the front pew of the Methodist church. They're not bad people, they're just so literal minded. Sometimes I just want to shake them. Thank God for the library, at least I can exercise my imagination.

JACK. You don't belong here.

SUSAN. And where do I belong?

JACK. New York.

SUSAN. Oh, Lord, you might as well say Shangri-La.

JACK. Why don't you go?

SUSAN. Just like that? Just pick up and go?

JACK. I did.

SUSAN. That's different. You're a man. I couldn't ... where would I live?

JACK. You could live with me. We'd get an apartment together in the Village.

SUSAN. Just like *My Sister Eileen*. I'd love to go to the Fifth Avenue Library — isn't that the one with the lions? — and just stand there, inhaling books, until Katherine Hepburn walks by. Is New York really as exciting as they say?

JACK. Better. Or it would be if you were there. Come with me and we'll light up the lights on Broadway. How does that sound?

JASON. Like catnip to a cat. Oh, you son-of-a-bitch, Jack.

SUSAN. I couldn't ... what would we live on?

JACK. Moonbeams and champagne.

SUSAN. Reality raises its ugly head once more. The only way I'll ever get to do anything is if someone just sweeps me away and doesn't let me think. Will you do that? Will you be my savior, Jack? *(Tense pause. Susan breaks it with a laugh.)* The farthest Dan and I ever get is to Kansas City. Last time we went to the Jewel Box. Do you know about it? The entertainers and half the audience are men dressed in women's clothes. I mean they do it surprisingly well, some of them are very pretty. It's all quite fun.

JACK. Was Mr. Hauser amused?

SUSAN. I wouldn't say amused, but he's a good sport about it. One of the singers came to our table and Dan invited him, her, to sit down and we all had a drink.

JACK. I wouldn't have thought that was Daniel's cup of tea.

SUSAN. Daniel is really very compassionate. He would never be rude to someone like that.

JACK. But he'd prosecute them.

SUSAN. If they misbehave.

JACK. Misbehave ... Susan, you are so innocent. Maybe that's why I love you so much.

SUSAN. Do you really, Jack? I never know when you're serious.

JACK. With a passion that knows its bounds. Never mess with the wife of the county attorney, no matter how charmingly innocent she is.

SUSAN. I've been married for eighteen years, how innocent can I be?

JACK. Marriage is the best protection ... How was your interview with Goldberg? Today was the big day, wasn't it?

SUSAN. *(Excitedly.)* He liked it!

JACK. I knew it! You're going to be a star!

SUSAN. He listened to the tape, he said I handled it very well — you know Walter Mason is not the easiest man to interview, I practically had to explain to him what the pyramids were. "Those pointy things in the sand ... "

JACK. You made him sound like a genius.

SUSAN. ... and he wants me to do it! He wants me to do a weekly show!

JACK. Fantastic.

SUSAN. *(Soberly.)* Now all I have to do is convince Daniel.

JACK. He won't stand in your way, why should he? Who wouldn't want to be married to the brightest light of Cascade?

SUSAN. I think he believes *I'm* married to the brightest light of Cascade.

JACK. Never mind, you'll work it out. There are always ways to get around a man.

SUSAN. Not Daniel.

JACK. Whisper to him in the bedroom. Use your womanly wiles.

SUSAN. Daniel is not susceptible to womanly wiles.

JACK. I can't imagine why not.

SUSAN. *(Said too much.)* Well, he's cerebral. *(Enter Jay and Luther Schmidt, "Smitty," a boy Jay's age.)*

JAY. I'm home.

SUSAN. Hello, Lambie. Come in and say hello to Mr. Stone. *(Jay walks directly to Jack; Smitty hangs back.)*

JAY. Hi.

SUSAN. Hi, who?

JACK. No, Susan ...

JAY. Hi, Mr. Stone.

JACK. Don't make him call me Mister. It makes me feel ancient. How you doing, Jay? *(Jack offers his hand, which Jay takes awkwardly.)*

JAY. Smitty and I are going to play some basketball at the Bedwells.

SUSAN. Luther, have you met Mr. Stone? *(Smitty hangs back, shyly.)* Come on in. *(Smitty drags in.)*

SUSAN. Jay, introduce your friend.

JAY. This is Smitty.

SUSAN. Is that the way I taught you?

JAY. Mr. Stone, this is Luther Schmidt. Luther, this is Mr. Stone. *(They shake hands.)*

JACK. *(Amused.)* Hi, Smitty. How you doing?

SMITTY. Okay.

JACK. They're a fine, strapping pair, Sue. We ought to yoke 'em up.

SUSAN. Sit down, boys. We'll have a talk.

JAY. What did I do now?

SUSAN. Nothing. I thought it would be nice to have some conversation. You're old enough.

JACK. Your mother wants to show you off.

JAY. God, Mom. Smitty doesn't want to have a conversation.

SMITTY. I don't mind. *(Jay shoots the traitor a look. The boys sit down and slouch.)*

JACK. Lord, teenagers. I'd just about forgotten. Now let's see, what's the question you hate most? What are you going to be when you grow up?

JAY. A lawyer, then a senator.

SUSAN. Or maybe a novelist.

JAY. Yeah, maybe.

JACK. Do you like to write?

JAY. Not much. But I like to read. *(Jason buries his head in his hands in disgust and embarrassment.)*

JACK. Who is your favorite author?

SMITTY. Mickey Spillane.

JAY. What do you know about it. At least I *can* read.

JACK. What about you, Smitty? What are your ambitions?

JAY. He's going to work in the creamery.

SUSAN. Luther's father is the foreman at the creamery.

JAY. He's going to make butter the rest of his life.

SMITTY. I'm going to be an anthropologist.

JACK. Really? Good for you.

JAY. An anthropologist! You never told me that. You're just saying that to make me look bad. You don't even know what it is, do you know what it is?

SMITTY. Not exactly.

JAY. He doesn't even know what it means.

SUSAN. I'll get you boys something to eat.

JAY. We're going to the Bedwells.

SUSAN. You entertain Jack. It won't hurt you to be polite for a while. Jack can tell you about basketball. He used to be a wonderful player. *(Susan exits to kitchen.)*

JACK. You don't want to talk about basketball, do you. The only thing I had on my mind at your age was sex. I had the same hard-on for five years. *(Jay and Smitty glance at one another, not sure whether to laugh or die of embarrassment.)* When I had to recite in class, I'd do it bent over, like my spine was deformed.

SMITTY. Jesus.

JACK. I'm not shocking you, am I? You've probably both got erections right now, haven't you?

SMITTY. Yeah.

JAY. God, Smitty!

SMITTY. Well, don't you?

JASON. Naturally.

JAY. No.

JACK. I tried to screw the cat once.

JAY. Jesus! My mom's in the kitchen!

SMITTY. Did you do it?

JACK. It wasn't a good idea.

SMITTY. I stuck it in my mom's cold cream jar once.

JAY. Smitty!

JACK. How was it?

SMITTY. Better than in the butter tubs at the creamery.

JAY. Do we have to talk about this?

JACK. What's the matter, Jay? Don't you ever do it?

JAY. I practice self-discipline.

SMITTY. We used to do it together. Remember when we did each
other in the john at North Street Texaco station?

JAY. I was just a kid then!

JACK. Nothing to be ashamed of, Jay. What are friends for? *(Susan
enters from kitchen, carrying a tray of snacks for the boys. There is a
sudden and deathly silence among the men.)*

SUSAN. Well, now, what am I interrupting?

JACK. Oh, man talk. You know.

JAY. We weren't talking about anything!

SUSAN. All right. Here, boys, eat up. They work up such an
appetite at this age.

JACK. Yes, I remember. *(Smitty chuckles.)*

SUSAN. I don't know what they do to burn off all that energy, but
I wish I could do it. *(Smitty laughs out loud.)*

JAY. Shut up!

SUSAN. What's going on here?

JAY. Nothing except I'm going to belt him if he doesn't shut up.

SUSAN. Now what is it? Jack, tell me!

JACK. Later, Sue. I don't want to embarrass the boys. *(Smitty
laughs again. Jay slugs him on the shoulder.)*

SUSAN. I should have known better than to expect them to act
civilized for ten minutes at a time.

JACK. We were just talking about girls. You know.

SUSAN. Ah. Did you ask Kate today, Jay?

JAY. No.

SUSAN. He's dying to ask this sweet girl to the junior prom, but he's too shy.

SMITTY. He's afraid to ask her because he can't dance.

JAY. What is it with you today!

JACK. You can't dance, Jay? Susan, you've neglected the boy's education.

SUSAN. I've offered to teach him a dozen times. He's too embarrassed to dance with his mother.

JAY. I can dance as much as I need to.

JACK. But Jay, dancing is so much more than just moving around. You can *say* things with your body.

SUSAN. He gets it from his father.

JACK. His loss is my gain. *(Jack stands before Susan, holds out his arms.)* This is called the dance of death, 'cause you could just die in my arms.

SUSAN. Well, we'll just have to see about that.

JACK. Said the girl to the sailor. *(Susan winks at Jay, rises to Jack's arms. Jay is mortified. Singing.)* "Oh, how we danced, on the night we were wed ... " *(Susan and Jack dance at a demure distance at first.)*

SUSAN. See, Jay? There's nothing to it. Left, right, left. Right, left, right.

JACK. La da, da da dee, da dee, da da deeeee ...

JAY. That's not how we dance.

SUSAN. Oh, I've seen how you dance. *(Susan pulls Jack to her and they dance with their arms wrapped tightly around one another in a parody of teenagers. But she is also taking delight in the contact with Jack. This goes on a bit longer than strictly necessary for demonstration purposes. Smitty looks at Jay with a leer. Jay hits Smitty on the shoulder again, angrily.)*

JAY. God, Mom. *(Susan breaks away from Jack.)*

SUSAN. *(Innocently.)* Well? Isn't that the way you do it? I was just showing you.

JAY. I'm not all that interested.

SUSAN. You should be. How do you ever expect to get along socially if you don't dance? Come on, it's your turn. *(Susan holds out her arms. Jay refuses.)* Do you want me to teach you, or do you want Jack?

JACK. I'll show Smitty. *(Jack takes Smitty, Susan grabs a reluctant Jay.)* I'll be the woman, you lead. One, two, three, one two, three, one, two, three ... *(Susan tries to maneuver Jay meanwhile. Jay does it with ill grace, but Jack and Smitty move around very well.)*

SUSAN. What could be worse than dancing with your mother?

JACK. That's good, Smitty!

JAY. He can't dance.

SUSAN. He seems to be.

JACK. "Oh, how we danced, on the night we were wed ... " *(Both couples continue to dance, Jack and Smitty with increasing ease.)* Now try this. *(Jack teaches Smitty some new moves which require closer contact. Susan and Jay quit dancing and watch. They end in a flourish, with Jack bending Smitty backwards.)*

SMITTY. I thought I was supposed to lead.

JACK. And so you are. *(They do the ending again, this time with Smitty bending Jack backwards. Jack laughs and applauds, as does Susan. Smitty looks proud and embarrassed. Jay doesn't know quite what to think.)*

SUSAN. Wonderful.

JAY. Yeah, you make a beautiful couple. Can we go now?

SUSAN. Oh, go ahead, go on. *(To Jack.)* It's like trying to civilize a baboon. Would you get those things for me? I'll make us a fresh pot of coffee. *(Susan and Jack exit into the kitchen. Jay and Smitty go to edge of set, which represents outside.)*

JAY. God, old people!

SMITTY. Yeah.

JAY. Dancing! What gets into them?

SMITTY. Yeah, your mom was really ...

JAY. What?

SMITTY. Nothing.

JAY. What were you going to say about my mom?

SMITTY. I forgot.

JAY. You were sure dancing around like a fairy in there.

SMITTY. I was just ...

JAY. Did you enjoy that? Wooo-wooo! ...

SMITTY. I didn't like it! It was your mom's idea.

JAY. Are you going to dance like that at the prom?

SMITTY. No.

JAY. Do you have a date yet?

SMITTY. I guess I'm going to take Elaine Gilchrist.

JAY. Pardon me while I barf.

SMITTY. I know. Don't tell anybody.

JAY. She looks like a beagle, you know that, don't you?

SMITTY. I know, I know.

JAY. She'll probably let you score with her, though, just out of gratitude.

SMITTY. You think so?!

JAY. She's a Catholic. They all put out … Of course your dick would rot off. *(Pause.)*

SMITTY. It might be worth it. I heard Catholics keep guns in the basement of the church.

JAY. That's right.

SMITTY. How come?

JAY. In case the Pope orders them to overthrow things. Smitty — what do you think of Jack Stone?

SMITTY. I think he's neat … I mean … I don't know. What do you think?

JAY. He sure doesn't act like he's thirty, does he? I just wish my mom wouldn't act so silly around him. Parents get so weird in public sometimes.

SMITTY. My dad sticks out his finger and if you pull it, he'll fart. *(Pause. Jay is appalled.)* Your dad doesn't do that?

JAY. My dad's a lawyer.

SMITTY. My dad's just joking.

JAY. Oh, neat joke. Does he do that while your mom is teaching you all those nifty fairy dance moves? *(Jay flaps his wings.)*

SMITTY. Well, at least my mom's not fucking Jack Stone. *(Jay leaps upon Smitty. They wrestle angrily. Jay easily ends up on top.)*

JAY. Take it back! Take it back!

SMITTY. I take it back. *(Jay gets up, leaving Smitty on the floor, and exits. After a moment, Smitty gets up.)* Jay. Don't be mad at me. *(Smitty exits after Jay.)*

JASON. I had never thought of my parents as being sexual until I discovered a box of condoms in my father's sock drawer. Nestled there behind the cuff links and under the handkerchiefs, not a solitary rubber, not a pair, but a whole box! I was filled with admiration for my old man — he bought in bulk! Of course, who he used them on I had no idea. I couldn't imagine him doing it with — Mom. Nor did I understand, until many years later, that the use of condoms instead of a diaphragm represented a skirmish lost. *(Jay enters, slouches onto sofa. Hauser enters, home from work.)* The condom king. *(Proudly.)* By the box.

HAUSER. Hello, Speedo.

JAY. Hi, Dad.

HAUSER. Where's your mother?

JAY. I think she went next door to visit with Jack's parents.

HAUSER. Her own personal reclamation case. She's going to have

Jack back on his feet and out of Cascade just as a matter of self-defense.

JAY. Don't you like Jack?

HAUSER. Sure I do, I'm only joking. Jack was a heck of a basketball player in his day. Lightning quick. And he was musical.

JAY. He still is. Did you win your case?

HAUSER. Yes.

JAY. You don't sound very happy.

HAUSER. It's not a happy chore, son, sending men to jail.

JAY. Why do you do it?

HAUSER. A society has rules just like a family, and some things, some behaviors, a family or a society just can't tolerate.

JAY. I learned to dance today.

HAUSER. Oh?

JAY. Jack and Mom demonstrated.

HAUSER. (Distractedly.) Dancing is a worthwhile pursuit, your mother has always told me. I never saw much point in it myself. But there are many different tastes.

JAY. Said the girl to the sailor ... Mom and Jack danced together, so Smitty and I could watch.

HAUSER. Yes?

JAY. He was singing ... They looked like they'd practiced.

HAUSER. Where was this?

JAY. Right here. In your house.

HAUSER. This looks like a good place for it.

JAY. Said the girl to the sailor.

HAUSER. What is that you keep saying?

JAY. It's what Jack says.

HAUSER. Don't you say it.

JAY. Is there anything wrong with it?

HAUSER. It's tiresome, annoying, and juvenile.

JAY. Dad ... what would you do if someone made a pass at Mom?

HAUSER. Like who?

JAY. I don't know. What difference does it make?

HAUSER. It makes a lot of difference. If it was a friend who'd had too much to drink, that's one thing ...

JAY. Like a sex maniac.

HAUSER. What would I do if a sex maniac made a pass at your mother? Is that what you're asking? I don't think sex maniacs make passes exactly. They attack.

JAY. Well what if she was attacked, then. What would you do?

21

HAUSER. Is the sex maniac armed?

JAY. God, Dad!

HAUSER. Well, it matters, Jay. It's a question of using reasonable force. If he has a weapon, I'd be justified … This isn't what you wanted to know, is it?

JAY. No.

HAUSER. I would do what I had to do, son. I would protect your mother. I would protect our family … What would you do?

JAY. I'd kill the son-of-a-bitch! *(Jay exits angrily.)*

HAUSER. Jay! Come back here! *(Jay does not return. Hauser is left to ponder the significance of the outburst. Hauser exits during the following.)*

JASON. I have reconstructed much of this story from things my parents didn't tell me. I didn't witness all of the events, only the results. And looking back, even now with hindsight honed by a generation of enlightenment, it is hard for me to place the blame for what happened. How much was mine? Some, but not as much as I thought at first. I was never as important as I assumed — a lesson that has come gratefully with the years. My mother? Some. Her flirtation was the catalyst and she was never as innocent as she thought. Jack? What was his charm? His apparent candor? He seemed so frank and open, although much of what he said was a lie. He dazzled us with the glint of a tin can in an empty field. But we responded. My father? … *(Sadly.)* My father — the righteousness was sincere — but willed. He wanted so much to do the right thing. To act the right way … He could not control what he felt. None of us could do that. *(Hauser enters, sipping a drink. He sits in a chair, musing. Jack enters, brightly.)*

JACK. Sue! Oh, Susan!

HAUSER. She's not here, Jack.

JACK. Oh, Dan. I knocked, but no one answered …

HAUSER. Sue's wopsing around at the radio station. She won't be home till after six.

JACK. I just came from the library, I brought her the book she wanted. Did you ever see anyone read as much? She must go through ten books a week.

HAUSER. She loves her stories. I've never acquired a taste for fiction. Novels seem so — I don't know. Futile, I guess. Maybe I see too much reality in a day to want to spend my evenings chasing great white whales.

JACK. I'll just leave the book — or should I bring it back later, or …

HAUSER. I'm glad you're here, Jack. We haven't had much chance to talk since you've been back.

JACK. I thought maybe you were avoiding me. *(Pause.)*

HAUSER. Maybe I have been. Will you join me in a drink?

JACK. I didn't know you drank.

HAUSER. I don't, usually. Sue likes a cocktail when we have friends over, but I don't normally bother. What would you like? This is bourbon.

JACK. Bourbon's fine.

HAUSER. You're not still in training.

JACK. For what?

HAUSER. Basketball.

JACK. Oh, good Lord. I wasn't good enough to play anywhere but Cascade. I haven't touched a basketball since high school. That's ten years.

HAUSER. That's a shame. I never saw anybody work harder at a game. I used to watch you out on your driveway, shooting baskets. Gloves on in the winter, shirt off and sweating in the summer. Day after day. I used to sit right here and watch, and then we'd go to all your high school games. You knew that, didn't you?

JACK. Yeah, I knew that. I didn't know you were watching from in here, though. That makes me feel kind of funny.

HAUSER. Someone is always watching, Jack. You should remember that … *(Pause.)* This tastes absolutely terrible, you know. You'd have to be very dedicated to acquire a taste for it.

JACK. What's the occasion? You're home early, aren't you?

HAUSER. One of the virtues of being the boss. Jay won't be home for a couple of hours. I enjoy having the house to myself once in a while … So tell me, Jack, how has your visit been? Have you enjoyed being home again?

JACK. *(Sarcastically.)* It's been terrific.

HAUSER. Nice and peaceful here in Cascade, isn't it? Just the thing for jangled nerves. Not like New York City.

JACK. No, it's certainly not like New York City. But then, what is?

HAUSER. Well, I don't know. I've never been to New York. That shows a rather provincial streak in my character, don't you think? Must be something wrong with me. After law school I just came right back here to Cascade and settled down. Sometimes I wonder just how good a lawyer I could have been, but I'm not going to find out here, no opportunities here.

JACK. Your job must have its satisfactions.

HAUSER. Oh, yes.

JACK. It must be very gratifying, keeping things neat and tidy.

HAUSER. Is that how you see it?

JACK. That's a good part of it, isn't it? You're sort of the fist of public morality, aren't you? Shine a bright light in all the little cracks and crevices, find those undesirables who don't like the light.

HAUSER. I don't always like it, you know. I don't do it for personal reasons. I won a case a few days ago, sent two pathetic little men to jail.

JACK. I heard.

HAUSER. They hadn't hurt anyone with their behavior but themselves. But they were stupid enough to be seen doing it. It's a practice we can't allow, as a society.

JACK. You would know better than I what society can allow. Me, I tend to think society should mind its own business.

HAUSER. Is that how they see it in New York City? *(Hauser pours himself another drink.)*

JACK. It works out that way.

HAUSER. Or are there simply more cracks and crevices to hide in in the big city? Another drink, Jack?

JACK. No.

HAUSER. *(Of the drink.)* It doesn't get any better, but it does get easier. You know, my choices were pretty ordinary. On purpose, I wanted to be ordinary. But you, you made some choices that defy analysis.

JACK. Oh, really?

HAUSER. Well, they seemed that way to us. You left so fast it was like hounds were at your heels. One day you graduate from high school, a bright young man with promise — the next day you're gone. Not just gone, practically disappeared. I can understand your leaving Cascade, but for a boy with all your promise to just get swallowed up in New York City …

JACK. I didn't disappear, I knew where I was at all times — or most of the time. Besides, I didn't have all that much promise in the first place.

HAUSER. A mystery.

JACK. Bright lights, big city. Lots of small town boys do it.

HAUSER. Not without a trace. You should have written, Jack. Your parents were very concerned. When they asked me to, I made some inquiries.

JACK. What kind of inquiries?

HAUSER. And of course I was curious myself. What happened to the boy who shot baskets day and night?

JACK. What does "making inquiries" mean?

HAUSER. I told your parents you were a healthy young man leading a bachelor's life in the big city. Of course, if you'd written more often, they wouldn't have been so concerned. I'm going to have to impress the importance of that upon Jay. I don't want his mother to worry when he goes away to school. Of course, she'll worry anyway. It's hard not to. A mother doesn't want her son snatched away by the first pretty girl who comes along. *(Pause.)* Tell me about *your* love life, Jack.

JACK. What about it?

HAUSER. What's it like with all those people to choose from and no constraints? It must keep you busy.

JACK. I've had a few lovers.

HAUSER. Lovers. That sounds pretty racy. A couple of men around here have mistresses, but that's about as exotic as we get. Lovers.

JACK. It may sound better than it is.

HAUSER. It sounds French. Very worldly, very sophisticated. You must be an expert at giving pleasure.

JACK. Not really.

HAUSER. You've given my wife great pleasure since you've been here. *(Pause.)*

JACK. I'm glad. *(Pause.)*

HAUSER. So am I.

JACK. I hope you don't misunderstand our relationship.

HAUSER. I hope so too.

JACK. Susan and I are friends.

HAUSER. Susan and I are friends, too. But I'm not terribly good at giving her pleasure. I'm not a dancer, for instance. Never got the knack of it. I feel like I'm stumbling and I can't ever quite catch the beat of the music.

JACK. Well, it's a learned skill.

HAUSER. I understand that you're good at teaching it.

JACK. Do you want a dancing lesson, Dan? Is that what this is all about?

HAUSER. No.

JACK. I can teach you my dance of death. *(Jack dances a few steps.)* I could teach you in a couple of minutes. Who knows, it might change your life.

HAUSER. I don't want to change my life. I value stability, it's essential for a serious life.

JACK. A serious life? Are some lives more serious than others?

HAUSER. Yours isn't. I told you, I made inquiries.

JACK. I will have another drink, if that's all right.

HAUSER. Sit down. *(Jack stops.)* Susan and I probably seem very different from each other — and we are. We may not have much in common except Jay — and the way we feel about each other. She's the best friend I've got in the world, the best I've ever had. I wouldn't want her to be misled into believing impossibilities. Just as I wouldn't want Jay subjected to the wrong influence at this point in his life.

JACK. *(Lightly.)* What are the wrong influences in Cascade?

HAUSER. You, I think.

JACK. *(Stunned.)* Me? Why?

HAUSER. You know why.

JACK. What have I done?

HAUSER. You're not the kind of influence Jay needs. Let's leave it at that.

JACK. But why?

HAUSER. Oh, stop it, Jack. Don't make me spell it out.

JACK. I swear to you, I've never done a thing …

HAUSER. I know about your incident in the Manhattan bus depot. *(Jack is felled, absolutely deflated.)*

JACK. Oh, God.

HAUSER. The police keep records of these things.

JACK. It wasn't that way. It was a mistake.

HAUSER. I was thorough in my inquiries. I wanted to be fair. You haven't been very discreet in New York, have you?

JACK. Oh, Jesus! *(Jack buries his face in his hands, overcome.)*

HAUSER. I don't understand how you could let yourself.

JACK. I wouldn't expect you to understand … Have you told my parents?

HAUSER. Not yet.

JACK. Please don't. Please.

HAUSER. I think I owe it to them.

JACK. No!

HAUSER. They'll learn eventually.

JACK. No, they won't. They don't want to. God, it would kill them! Please don't tell them.

HAUSER. I've known your parents most of my life. I don't know what they ever did to deserve this.

JACK. *(Bitterly.)* Me, you mean. I'm not something anyone deserves. I'm just nature's cruel little joke.

HAUSER. *Why,* Jack?

JACK. It's the way I am.

HAUSER. You are what you make of yourself. Don't give in to the urge.

JACK. Give in? I'm already there! It's who I am.

HAUSER. Your life is a result of your will.

JACK. You're not going to try and "cure" me, are you?

HAUSER. I don't honestly know what I should do.

JACK. Mr. Hauser, please ... You can do whatever you want to me, I don't care, it's all been done already ... I don't know what to offer you, but if the memory of the kid next door who used to play basketball means anything to you, then please let my parents keep that memory, too. Don't tell them. Don't tell them.

HAUSER. I've handled this badly. I'm sorry. I didn't mean to humiliate you.

JACK. What did you mean to do? What do you want from me!?

HAUSER. I don't want anything from you, Jack. I won't tell your parents.

JACK. *(With relief.)* Thank you.

HAUSER. I don't want to hurt you.

JACK. Thank you. A lot of people do want to hurt me, as if it's their right. Thank you. *(Jack touches Hauser's hand in a gesture of gratitude. Hauser pulls away uncomfortably.)*

HAUSER. Don't get all het up about it.

JACK. We're all high-strung, didn't you know that? We get "het up" so easily. *(Very affected voice.)* Just the slightest little thing and away we soar. Tinkerbell and Peter Pan. And what was Peter's problem, anyway? The Island of Lost Boys? Now really.

HAUSER. *(Sharply.)* Stop that. At least have some respect for yourself.

JACK. Self-respect is difficult when you're an official object of hatred.

HAUSER. Stop dramatizing yourself. I don't hate you. I don't think most people do, they just feel embarrassed when they're around one of you.

JACK. Embarrassed?

HAUSER. I don't know quite how to act. You make most people uncomfortable. I don't know what to talk about.

JACK. Talk about anything. Talk about the crops. It doesn't have to be sex, does it?

HAUSER. It seems dishonest to ignore it. I mean, that's what you are.

JACK. Oh, like calling a spade a spade, or "Hello, I notice you're a Jew. Too bad."

HAUSER. I'd be a hypocrite to pretend those differences don't matter. But I don't discriminate against anyone.

JACK. God, the burden of superiority.

HAUSER. And it's not really their fault. That's how they were born, they can't do anything about it.

JACK. And "we" can?

HAUSER. Have you ever tried, Jack? Have you ever denied yourself? ... You don't look that way. No one would know.

JACK. I can "pass." Most of us can, we have to keep our jobs.

HAUSER. What do you mean, "most" of you?

JACK. I mean most of us are well-camouflaged. It's a survival instinct we learn early. *(Pause.)*

HAUSER. You're not saying most of "you" are normal-seeming guys?

JACK. We look surprisingly like real people. You might pass us on the street and say hello, even here in Cascade.

HAUSER. You make it sound like there are a lot of you.

JACK. Many. Farmers and accountants and husbands and fathers.

HAUSER. Husbands and fathers?

JACK. Shocking, isn't it?

HAUSER. How do you know?

JACK. Because I've held them in my arms for a few minutes before they went back to being husbands and fathers. Does that embarrass you?

HAUSER. ... How can they?

JACK. Because they have to.

HAUSER. But ... people can tell. Surely people can tell.

JACK. How? Do you think we wear dresses or pink stars on our foreheads?

HAUSER. Is there some way *you* can tell?

JACK. Only the secret password. "Hi, sailor!"

HAUSER. How do you meet? How do you find each other?

JACK. There's no system! We live like spies in enemy territory. You can't imagine the humiliation of being wrong about someone. Sometimes we'll circle each other for days, afraid to make the first move.

HAUSER. What are you afraid of?

JACK. Do you know what it feels like to have someone spit in your face? It burns forever. *(Pause.)*

HAUSER. Then how do you ever dare to reach out?

JACK. *(Facetiously.)* Where there's a will ...

HAUSER. I'm serious, Jack. How do you ever meet someone if you don't know? How can you be sure?

JACK. I can't wait to be sure before I live my life.

HAUSER. So what does that leave you? The bus depot? Do you go into a men's room and look at people until someone responds?

JACK. I'm leaving. *(Hauser stops him, somewhat roughly.)*

HAUSER. I want to know!

JACK. Why? So you can prosecute me? Or does this titillate you? ... *(Pause.)* You really want a dancing lesson after all, don't you?

HAUSER. I'm not going to prosecute anyone. You haven't committed any crimes — at least not in my jurisdiction.

JACK. *(Softer now.)* So what do you want to know, Dan? I did know you were watching me, you know. All those afternoons.

HAUSER. No, you didn't.

JACK. I sensed your eyes on me every day. Do you know how that made me feel? ... I was glad it was you. I tried to put a little something extra into it, because it was you ... Of course, at that age, I didn't fully understand why you were watching.

HAUSER. You were ... just basketball.

JACK. I'll show you what you want to know, Dan. I call it the dance of death because you could just die in my arms. *(Jack begins a slow, sinuous, seductive movement. This "dance," which continues to the end of the scene, is altogether sexier than the dancing he has done earlier. Sings softly.)* "Oh, how we danced ... " *(Spoken.)* If I met someone I liked I'd look into his eyes. Not that you can really tell anything that way. People lie with their eyes as much as with their words. Right now, for instance, I'm not sure what I see in your eyes. Compassion? ... Curiosity? ... Lust? *(Sings.)* " ... On the night we were wed ... " *(Spoken.)* I'd ask him to dance, and if he was like me, his throat would be tight, he'd have trouble breathing, he'd be shaking as if he were freezing, but he'd take my hands, and he would come to me, because this was what he wanted, this was what he needed. This was what he needed. *(Jack holds out his hands to Hauser. Seductively.)* Let me teach you to dance, Dan. *(Jack stands in front of Hauser, swaying gently, arms out.)* You can't go your whole life without it.

HAUSER. *(Weakly.)* No.

JACK. Come. Come to me. *(Jack takes Hauser's hands in his.)*

HAUSER. *(Weakly.)* Please don't.

JACK. I won't do anything you don't want me to. It's not too late to run, Dan ... Or come to me. *(Hauser stands, a bit unsteadily.)*

JASON. Run! *Run!*

JACK. *(Sings.)* "Oh, how we danced ... " It's so easy. It's so good. *(Jack touches Hauser's arm.)*

HAUSER. *(Huskily.)* Please don't. *(Jack places Hauser's hand on Jack's waist.)*

JACK. Nothing easier, nothing better. *(Hauser trembles.)*

HAUSER. Please.

JACK. It's too late to run. *(Jack places Hauser's arms around Hauser's body. Hauser trembles and sighs.)*

HAUSER. *(Strangled.)* Oh, God!

JACK. My Lord, how long have you been waiting? *(Hauser begins towards bedroom, he turns to Jack who follows.)*

JASON. He could have run! He could have run! *(Lights dim, time passes. Jay enters from "outside," bearing schoolbooks.)*

JAY. I'm home ... Anybody here? *(Jay flops onto sofa.)*

JASON. I was home an hour early because of a teacher's convention.

JAY. *(Lifting his head.)* Mom?

JASON. Stay there!

JAY. Mom, is that you?

JASON. Stay there!

JAY. Mom? Mom? *(Jay exits toward Jack and Hauser. Jason sags, defeated, as lights dim to black.)*

End of Act One

ACT TWO

The following morning. Jason enters.

JASON. In those days, such a short time ago, we still had blanks on our sociological maps, large uncharted territories marked "Here be Dragons." We knew so little about the creatures that lived there, and so, as with any unknown, we peopled the blanks with our own worst fears, creating monsters and two headed beasts with powers of enticement and defilement vastly beyond our own powers of resistance. We were superior to them, of course, but, with the illogic of a nightmare, they could bring us to ruin if we approached too closely. As I grew older, I began to realize that the warm embrace of a small town could smother as well as comfort. As Jack already knew, I learned there was no place to hide. The land was so flat that an Indian legend said it was the place the Creator sat while molding the rest of the world. And the spiritual landscape was flatter still. The community watched the antics of its members — or I thought it did — with the same unblinking stare as the all-seeing eye of God. I felt this way partly because everything I did was eventually reported back to my parents. I felt this was partly because I was a teenager and aching to revolt in some way that would have deep significance for me — but no serious repercussions. And I felt this way partly because it was the great, unalterable truth of my life in Cascade — there was no room for deviation. But mostly now I felt this way because I had something unspeakable to hide. *(Susan enters, makes preparations to the breakfast table. She exits into kitchen. Hauser enters and sits at the table. Susan enters, pauses momentarily when she sees Hauser, then continues laying the table. He looks at her expectantly, wants to speak, cannot. She avoids looking at him directly.)*
SUSAN. I have pancakes. They're almost ready.
HAUSER. I'm not very hungry.
SUSAN. You still have to eat.
HAUSER. I have a headache.
SUSAN. Alcohol does that. Was the sofa too uncomfortable?
HAUSER. I didn't sleep very much. *(She exits into the kitchen. After*

a moment she returns with pancakes which she puts in front of him.)

HAUSER. That's too much for me. Give it to Jay. Jay! Rise and shine!

SUSAN. He's not here. He left around six this morning.

HAUSER. Where did he go?

SUSAN. He didn't want to see you. *(Hauser is stunned, hurt.)*

HAUSER. He told you that?

SUSAN. You'll have to get your own dinner tomorrow. I'm starting my job for Mr. Goldberg.

HAUSER. I thought we were going to hold off on that.

SUSAN. After tomorrow I'll arrange my work schedule so that I'll be able to fix your meals. I don't want you to be inconvenienced.

HAUSER. I don't think we agreed you were going to do it.

SUSAN. Are you forbidding me?

HAUSER. You must make up your own mind.

SUSAN. He said if I enjoy it, there are other jobs there. He might be able to use me full-time.

HAUSER. Susan … *(Susan exits into kitchen. She enters with more pancakes which she adds to the stack on his plate.)*

SUSAN. There's toast coming.

HAUSER. Will you stop feeding me? Sit down, please. *(Susan sits, tentatively, on the edge of the seat.)* It's hard enough without all this.

SUSAN. I am so sorry. *(She sits erectly, folds hands demurely in her lap.)*

HAUSER. You know I don't drink very often … *(Susan gets to her feet. He reaches out to stop her, touches her arm, she pulls away as if burned.)* Susan, please.

SUSAN. Don't touch me! Do you know how that makes me feel now?

HAUSER. Let me explain.

SUSAN. I have to get your breakfast. *(Susan steps towards kitchen. He rises, stands in her way. She picks up the platter from the table.)* It will burn.

HAUSER. Let it burn, it doesn't matter.

SUSAN. Don't tell me it doesn't matter! It's what I do! *(She slams the platter onto the table. It breaks. Hauser stands silently. After a moment, Susan recovers herself.)* My mother gave us this platter. *(She starts to pick up the pieces as if the plate can be repaired. Hauser kneels to help her.)*

HAUSER. Maybe it can be fixed.

SUSAN. No.

HAUSER. It can be glued.

SUSAN. No. It's ruined.

HAUSER. We can do it.

SUSAN. No! *(She hurls the pieces that they have collected. Hauser pauses, then begins to pick up the pieces on his hands and knees. His back is to Susan. She crosses behind him, stops and strikes him on the back with her fist, furiously. Hauser turns, more startled than hurt. Susan has raised her fist to hit him again, but seeing his face she cannot hurt him.)* Do I repel you?

HAUSER. No!

SUSAN. Am I ugly to you?

HAUSER. You're beautiful!

SUSAN. I know I look older.

HAUSER. I love your looks, I love you ...

SUSAN. I'm not as pretty as I used to be.

HAUSER. It wasn't about that.

SUSAN. Maybe if I try harder ...

HAUSER. It had nothing to do with you.

SUSAN. You can't be that stupid! How do you think it makes me feel!

HAUSER. I wouldn't hurt you ...

SUSAN. Am I *so* ugly?

HAUSER. ... not for the world.

SUSAN. What do you need, Dan?

HAUSER. It wasn't about you.

SUSAN. Do I have to get you drunk?

HAUSER. Susan, I love you, I love you.

SUSAN. I have tried so hard — you're never interested.

HAUSER. I know ... I'm not ...

SUSAN. I feel like ...

HAUSER. I'm sorry, I'm sorry ...

SUSAN. What's wrong with me?

HAUSER. God, it's not you!

SUSAN. Then what is it! Dan! *(Pause.)* Was Jay lying? Was he mistaken?

HAUSER. It wasn't the way it looked ... It ... God, I can't talk about it.

SUSAN. You can always explain everything else.

HAUSER. I am so ashamed.

SUSAN. You have to give me something, Dan.

HAUSER. Don't hate me, Sue. Please, God, don't hate me. *(Pause.)*

SUSAN. I just want to understand.

HAUSER. I don't understand it.

SUSAN. I have to know where I am.

HAUSER. The same, the same! It doesn't change us. *(Susan is silent.)* I can't lose you, I can't lose my family! *(Pause.)* Please say something.

SUSAN. How could you let it happen?

HAUSER. I don't know, it just ... I don't know, I don't *know*.

SUSAN. How could you let yourself?

HAUSER. I'll do anything, anything. I can't lose you.

SUSAN. *Tell* me.

HAUSER. I can't even look at you. Please. Please. Forgive me. Susan. I swear to you, nothing like that will ever happen again.

SUSAN. How do I know that?

HAUSER. You know me, you know the kind of man I am.

SUSAN. I'm not sure I do anymore.

HAUSER. I'm the same person!

SUSAN. Are you?

HAUSER. Tell me what to say. Tell me what to do.

SUSAN. You always know the right thing to do. *(Pause.)* Tell me it didn't happen.

HAUSER. It wasn't me doing it. It was like I was watching it.

SUSAN. Was it the alcohol?

HAUSER. I'm not used to drinking, I had so much ...

SUSAN. You must have been drunk.

HAUSER. I was. I was.

SUSAN. Most of the bottle was gone.

HAUSER. I never drink that much.

SUSAN. Jack had been drinking, too ...

HAUSER. He started dancing.

SUSAN. Yes, he does that.

HAUSER. He called it his dance of death.

SUSAN. He does flatter himself.

HAUSER. He wanted me to dance with him.

SUSAN. I'm surprised either one of you could stand up.

HAUSER. Jack wasn't drunk.

SUSAN. He must have been or it wouldn't have happened.

HAUSER. No. He's that way.

SUSAN. Jack?

HAUSER. Yes.

SUSAN. I can't believe it!

HAUSER. He is.

SUSAN. He seems so ... I'm sorry, I don't understand that.

HAUSER. I've known it.

SUSAN. He can't be … *(Hauser nods.)* And I trusted him … Oh, that filthy man. He got you drunk and … it's disgusting.

HAUSER. *(Weakly.)* It wasn't … *(Hauser shakes his head, Susan doesn't notice this faint demurral.)*

SUSAN. Now I see.

HAUSER. *(Weakly.)* I just … I wasn't in control.

SUSAN. His poor parents! *(With strength.)* All right. I understand. You're not to blame, Dan.

HAUSER. I couldn't bear to lose you or Jay.

SUSAN. You're not going to lose us! We couldn't bear to lose you, either.

HAUSER. I don't know how to explain to Jay … I don't think I can ever … what he saw! What will he think of me?

SUSAN. He'll understand, I'll make him understand.

HAUSER. I should do it.

SUSAN. No. You'll overexplain. Leave Jay to me.

HAUSER. I need both of you so badly. *(Susan goes to him, puts her arm on him.)*

SUSAN. We need you, too.

HAUSER. I love you, Susan. *(He takes her hand, touches her face.)*

SUSAN. I love you, too. *(He clutches her to him, touches her suggestively. Surprised.)* Dan.

HAUSER. Jay's gone, isn't he? *(Hauser leads her towards bedroom.)*

SUSAN. You don't have to do this.

HAUSER. I want you, Sue. I want you.

SUSAN. *(With a laugh.)* We-ell. *(They exit affectionately.)*

JASON. I am married myself now, and I know the easy complicity marriage partners use — need to use — to present a united front to the world. And I know the price they pay for it. I didn't see my parents as truly human, then, of course — nor did they want me to. Selective blindness is one of a family's necessary deceptions. But the danger of encouraging our children to see us as godlike is that they will never forgive us once they learn the truth. *(Susan and Jay enter during above and remove table setting from preceding scene and set table anew.)*

SUSAN. No, Jay, the fork goes on the left side with the napkin. Spoon and knife on the right. I know you would think the big knife would be on the outside to protect the little spoon, but that isn't the way it works.

JAY. What difference does it make?

SUSAN. It matters how you do things, because your behavior tells who you are.

JASON. Throw your shoulders back.

JAY. People know who I am already …

SUSAN. Well, Smitty maybe. For the rest of us, the jury's out. There's a lot more to life than you'll find in Cascade, you know.

JASON. *(Sadly.)* No, Mom. Not really.

SUSAN. Do you think John Cheever chews gum when he goes into the offices of *The New Yorker?*

JAY. Everybody chews gum.

SUSAN. Believe me, Jay, everybody does not chew gum and some day you're going to meet a girl and she'll take you to meet her family and if you have a wad of gum in your mouth like some kind of talking cow — well, I'll be humiliated, and so will you. People judge you by those things.

JAY. No, they don't.

JASON. Oh, you would know …

SUSAN. Someday you'll see that I'm right and you'll be glad that I taught you the proper way to do things.

JAY. Nobody else does things the way you do.

SUSAN. Then you'll be different, and someday you'll be proud that you're different. Lambie, I only tell you these things because I love you. You know that, don't you? I love you more than anyone in the world, and I want the best for you.

JAY. More than anyone?

SUSAN. More than anyone. Now get rid of that gum before your father sees it.

JAY. I don't care if he does see it.

SUSAN. Now you listen to me, young man. I want you to make up with your father.

JAY. I won't.

SUSAN. He worships you, Jay. You're breaking his heart.

JAY. I'm not going to.

SUSAN. You're going to have to speak to him sometime.

JAY. You don't know how I feel, Mom.

SUSAN. I think I do. But you're not making matters any better by refusing to talk to him.

JAY. I've got nothing to say to him if he'd let himself get drunk like that. And he's got nothing to say I want to hear.

SUSAN. Lambie, listen to me. We're still a family, that's the main thing. We still have to stay together and support each other.

JAY. He's not in my family!

SUSAN. He's your father.

JAY. Make him leave! Make him go away! We don't need him! We could live together, just the two of us.

SUSAN. Now, stop this, Jay.

JAY. We can do it, Mom! You can work at the radio station, I can get a job, I'm tired of school anyway, I'm tired of this town, we could get out of here.

SUSAN. You'll be leaving here soon enough, you know I don't expect you to stay once you go to college. In the meantime, I don't want to hear any silly talk about quitting school.

JAY. I hate it here.

SUSAN. How do you think I feel about it? You don't even know this town yet. Jay, it's where we find ourselves, your father loves it here, we have to learn to deal with it.

JAY. What if someone finds out!

SUSAN. Jay ...

JAY. I'm serious. Someone's bound to find out. Do you know what would happen to me at school?

SUSAN. No one is going to find out because we're not going to tell them.

JAY. What if Jack tells somebody?

SUSAN. Jack isn't going to tell anybody, believe me.

JAY. What if he gets arrested and they make him talk?

SUSAN. Now you're being silly.

JAY. I'm not! That's the kind of thing that happens.

SUSAN. Now why would he get arrested?

JAY. For anything. What's with Jack, anyway? I thought he liked you. I thought you liked him.

SUSAN. No. I was just being friendly because of his parents. They've been wonderful neighbors for years.

JAY. Why would he let Dad act like that?

SUSAN. Your father didn't do it. Jack made him.

JAY. God, why?

SUSAN. Jack's that way.

JAY. You mean ... Jack?

SUSAN. Apparently that's what he's like.

JAY. I thought they were drunk? You mean he's ... What do you mean, Mom?

SUSAN. You're old enough, I don't have to spell everything out for you.

JAY. You mean he does that … all the time?

SUSAN. Apparently.

JAY. Jesus! Why?

SUSAN. I don't know, Jay. I don't know why men do most of the things they do. You tell me.

JAY. Me! I don't know anything about it!

SUSAN. I didn't mean to say it that way.

JAY. Jesus, let's get out of here. I'll take care of you, Mom. We could go to Omaha. You can count on me, I swear.

SUSAN. Now, stop all this, Lambie. *(Jay pulls away rejected.)*

JAY. Don't call me Lambie.

SUSAN. Don't be angry with me.

JAY. *(Angrily.)* I'm not.

SUSAN. I've let you down too.

JAY. No, you haven't. You haven't let anyone down, Mom.

SUSAN. Do you think I'm a good mother at least?

JAY. You're the best. *(Susan beckons him into an embrace, which he submits to.)*

SUSAN. Can I count on you, Jay? Can I trust in you?

JAY. You know you can, Mom.

SUSAN. You don't think I'm old and ugly, do you?

JAY. I think you're beautiful. Everybody does.

SUSAN. *(Pause.)* Then if you won't get rid of that gum for your father, do it for me. *(Jay removes gum as they exit into kitchen.)*

JASON. How many years of beneficent deception do your parents owe you? My father had managed sixteen for me — was I short changed? When you do see your parents at last, you see them with the eyes that they have trained to see. Who is to blame for that? … *(Jay and Smitty enter.)*

JAY. *(Calling.)* I'm home! … Mom! … Mom!

SMITTY. Maybe she's not at home.

JAY. *(Noise of an idiot.)* Duh! … She's at work.

SMITTY. Your mom's got a job?

JAY. Not a job, she doesn't have to work. She's doing it because she wants to.

SMITTY. You wouldn't catch me working if I didn't have to.

JAY. I wouldn't catch you if you were gonorrhea.

SMITTY. What did I do?

JAY. Nothing.

SMITTY. If I did something, tell me. I'll apologize.

JAY. You pounded your pud once too often and it stunted your brain. Are you sorry for that?

SMITTY. You want me to go home?

JAY. I don't care what you do.

SMITTY. You're so touchy lately. What's going on?

JAY. Nothing's going on!

SMITTY. Is it this trouble with your parents?

JAY. Jesus Christ, will you shut up!

SMITTY. You can tell me, Jay.

JAY. Oh, I suppose, I suppose I can tell you.

SMITTY. You can. I'd never tell if you told me not to. They could do anything to me, pull out my fingernails, you know the way the Japs do? I wouldn't talk.

JAY. That's because you've got no brains. Let them pull out your fingernails? You're stupid, Smitty. You're really stupid. How would you scratch your ass without fingernails? *(Pause.)*

SMITTY. Did you ask Katie to the prom yet?

JAY. She's a scag. I'm not asking anybody.

SMITTY. Great! I won't either. We can go together.

JAY. Some date.

SMITTY. *(Sympathetically.)* To hell with them. We don't need the girls. *(Smitty puts an arm around Jay's shoulder in an attempt to cheer him up. Jay leaps at the touch.)*

JAY. What the hell do you mean by that! What the hell do you mean?

SMITTY. I didn't mean anything.

JAY. You're good at dancing with men, aren't you? You know why nobody likes you? You know why you don't have any friends? Because you're weird, that's why.

SMITTY. Oh, eat me.

JAY. You'd love that, wouldn't you. *(Jay crosses towards exit.)*

SMITTY. Where are you going?

JAY. I'm going to the bathroom to take a Smitty. *(Jay exits.)*

SMITTY. I'm not going to stay if I'm not wanted. *(Smitty returns to the sofa and flops down again. Hauser enters with briefcase. Smitty sits bolt upright.)*

HAUSER. Ah, Smitty, old sock, old shoe.

SMITTY. Yes, sir.

HAUSER. And how, exactly, do matters proceed with you, Master Smitty?

SMITTY. Huh?

HAUSER. How's it going?

SMITTY. Fine.

HAUSER. Where's Jay?

SMITTY. He's weeing.

HAUSER. And you? Studying, I see.

SMITTY. Mr. Hauser, can I ask you a question?

HAUSER. If it's not too taxing. I've had a rather hard day.

SMITTY. Let's say I was arrested for something I didn't do.

HAUSER. Like what?

SMITTY. Murder.

HAUSER. Why were you arrested?

SMITTY. Let's say someone managed to put my fingerprints on the murder weapon. Like in that movie? So, my question is, would they give me the electric chair even though I was innocent?

HAUSER. I'm afraid so, Smitty.

SMITTY. Jeez! I knew it!

HAUSER. I'm only teasing you, son. If you're innocent, and I believe you truly are, you have nothing to fear. Now let me ask you a question.

SMITTY. Sure.

HAUSER. Has Jay said anything to you about the little problem we're having?

SMITTY. I know he's not talking to you.

HAUSER. Did he tell you why?

SMITTY. No, sir.

HAUSER. You must have been curious. You must have asked.

SMITTY. He just said he didn't want to talk about it. I had a fight with my dad once. I wouldn't worry about it, Mr. Hauser. It's just something kids go through.

HAUSER. I know your father.

SMITTY. Yes, sir. He knows you, too.

HAUSER. We see each other at all the ball games. He's a good man, a hard worker. I've heard his employer at the creamery speak well of him. You can be proud of your father, Smitty. Remember that.

SMITTY. Yes, sir.

HAUSER. It's important for a boy to be proud of his father ... Smitty, will you tell Jay something for me? I'm having a little trouble getting through to him right now. Will you tell him?

SMITTY. Sure.

HAUSER. Tell him I love him. *(Smitty laughs nervously.)* Will you tell him that?

SMITTY. Okay. *(Jay enters, sees his father, immediately exits again.*

Hauser and Smitty both see him.)
HAUSER. How did you and your father end your fight?
SMITTY. He took off his belt and told me if I didn't quit being such a horse's ass he'd beat the peewaden out of me.
HAUSER. *(Laughs.)* I think Jay's a little too big. *(Hauser crosses to exit.)* You'll remember to tell him. *(Calling.)* You can come out now, Jay. I'm leaving. *(Hauser exits. After a moment, Jay enters.)*
JAY. What the hell were you doing!
SMITTY. Nothing.
JAY. You were talking to my father, I heard you. I told you I'm not talking to him.
SMITTY. Well, I'm not you.
JAY. Did he say why I'm not talking to him?
SMITTY. No, I'm not sure he even knows.
JAY. Oh, he knows. What were you talking about?
SMITTY. The electric chair. And he said to tell you he loves you.
JAY. He said that to you? God!
SMITTY. I like your father.
JAY. What do you know about it? ... He actually said that? *(Hauser enters.)*
HAUSER. You boys want something to eat? *(Jay stiffens, ignores his father, but does not leave.)*
SMITTY. No thank you, Mr. Hauser.
HAUSER. How are you, Jay? *(Jay sits in sullen silence.)* You left the car awfully low on gas last night. I'd appreciate it if you'd try to keep the tank moist, at least. *(Hauser waits for a response, Jay ignores him.)* Well ...
SMITTY. Why don't you sit down, Mr. Hauser. *(Jay gives Smitty a murderous look.)*
HAUSER. Thank you, Smitty. I think I will. *(Hauser sits down. All three sit there uncomfortably for a moment.)*
SMITTY. Can I ask you another question?
HAUSER. Sure.
SMITTY. Is it true that if I take a date over the state line into Kansas I can go to jail?
HAUSER. What are you talking about?
SMITTY. That's what Jay told me. I knew that was crazy.
JAY. *(To Hauser.)* The Mann Act! You told me yourself.
HAUSER. Ah. Well, the Mann Act makes it a federal crime to transport a woman across state lines for immoral purposes, but that doesn't apply to Smitty.

JAY. Why else would he take a date to Kansas?

HAUSER. *(Laughs.)* The law is intended to fight prostitution.

SMITTY. *(Aghast.)* Why?

JAY. You're so dumb.

SMITTY. So ... why?

JAY. Public policy. *(Looks at Hauser.)* Right?

HAUSER. Right. *(Susan enters from work.)*

SUSAN. Well, what's this happy little group?

JAY. Hi, Mom.

SMITTY. Hello.

HAUSER. Hello, Susan. *(He approaches her tentatively.)* We were just talking.

SUSAN. All of you?

HAUSER. *(Very pleased.)* A regular roundtable discussion. How are you, sweetheart? *(He holds out his arms, somewhat tentatively, and she, also tentatively, steps into them.)*

SUSAN. I interviewed Coach Henderson today about the prospects for the basketball season.

HAUSER. Was it a good interview?

SUSAN. I assume he instructs by example, not vocabulary.

HAUSER. I think the boys are hungry.

SUSAN. Good. Why don't you come into the kitchen and talk while I fix you something to eat. Hello, Luther.

SMITTY. Hello. *(Susan and Smitty exit into the kitchen. Jay retrieves schoolbooks and goes into the kitchen followed by Hauser.)*

JASON. Our home had been shaken and so we built a new one, made of straw, and pretended it was as strong as before. Who can blame us, we needed shelter and we used what was at hand ... The strong wind blew on the third day. *(Smitty and Jay hurry in, agitated, excited.)*

SMITTY. Jesus, Jay.

JAY. That son-of-a-bitch!

SMITTY. Jesus!

JAY. Pow! *(Smitty shadowboxes.)*

SMITTY. Boom!

JAY. The son-of-a-bitch!

SMITTY. You really hit him.

JAY. He's lucky I didn't knock his head off.

SMITTY. I'm surprised he didn't fall down. I'm surprised you didn't knock him out.

JAY. I hit him hard enough, but you have to catch them right on the tip of the chin to knock them out. He moved a little.

SMITTY. Or if you hit them on the temple, you can shatter their brain case. *(Smitty looks out the window.)*

JAY. *(With some concern.)* Is he still out there?

SMITTY. No, he's gone.

JAY. I'd kick his ass if he wasn't.

SMITTY. Wham! God, Jay. I've never hit anybody in my life. I mean, not in the face.

JAY. Sometimes you have to.

SMITTY. I guess! ... Why?

JAY. What do you mean, why?

SMITTY. Did he say something I didn't hear?

JAY. Christ, you're stupid.

SMITTY. I know, but what did he say?

JAY. He's a homo.

SMITTY. Jack Stone?

JAY. Everybody knows that. I don't want him around this house. Would you?

SMITTY. God, no. *(Hauser and Susan enter.)*

HAUSER. Ah-ha, a gathering of the brain trust. How are you doing, Smitty?

SMITTY. Hello, Mr. Hauser. Hello, Mrs. Hauser.

SUSAN. Hello, Luther.

HAUSER. Hi, Jay.

SUSAN. Hello, Lambie.

JAY. Hi.

HAUSER. What have you two been up to? Still working on world peace?

SMITTY. I have to go home now. I'll call you, Jay. *(Jay nods.)* Goodbye.

SUSAN. Goodbye, Luther.

HAUSER. You don't have to run on our account, Smitty. *(Smitty exits.)*

SUSAN. That boy always makes me feel better about myself by comparison. *(Not very sincerely.)* That was mean of me, I'm sorry.

HAUSER. Old Smitty's not so bad — if your expectations aren't too high. Isn't that right, Jay?

JAY. How come you're home together?

HAUSER. I stopped by the radio station to watch your mother interview Hope and Crosby.

SUSAN. Bing couldn't make it, so I talked to the Schrag boy who won the National Merit Scholarship instead.

JAY. That's not very nice, making fun of her.

HAUSER. I'm just teasing, son.

JAY. You're not exactly Clarence Darrow, you know.

HAUSER. *(Momentarily shocked.)* Well, I try ... But I see your point.

SUSAN. It's all right, Jay. I don't mind a little teasing.

HAUSER. I'm glad to see you stick up for your mother, Jay. That's a good quality. A little misplaced, maybe. You don't need to defend her from me. We're a team.

JAY. I saw your friend, Jack, outside when I came home today.

SUSAN. Oh?

HAUSER. *(One eye on Susan.)* I ran into the Sergeant-at-Arms from the Lion's Club on the street today. Do you remember him, Jay? At last year's father-and-son banquet he fined me a dollar because you weren't wearing a tie?

JAY. I told him not to come sneaking around here anymore.

HAUSER. The father-and-son banquet is next week. If you walk over at lunchtime, I'll drive you back to school afterwards.

JAY. Okay.

HAUSER. And Jay, it might be cheaper on me if you wear a tie.

JAY. I hit him.

SUSAN. Jack?

HAUSER. *(Slowly.)* Why?

JAY. He mouthed off to me. I hit him in the face. I nearly killed him.

HAUSER. Is he all right?

JAY. He's lucky he's still walking.

SUSAN. Are you hurt, Jay?

JAY. Me? Shiiit.

HAUSER. Jay!

JAY. Sorry, Mom.

HAUSER. What did he say to you?

JAY. Just homo stuff. Bam!

HAUSER. Sit down and tell me about it.

JAY. There's nothing to tell. I told him to go away and he gave me one of those looks so I ... *(Pounds fist into his palm.)*

HAUSER. Sit *down!* *(Jay, startled, sits.)* Now, what exactly did he say?

JAY. Homo talk.

HAUSER. Stop using that word. What did he say?

JAY. I don't remember, okay? I can't tell you in front of Mom.

HAUSER. Sue, perhaps you'd better ...

SUSAN. I'm staying.

HAUSER. Go ahead, Jay.

JAY. Well ... he didn't actually say anything, but he gave me one of those looks.

HAUSER. "Those looks ... " What kind of look? Describe the look.

SUSAN. Dan, he's not on the witness stand. Just tell us so we can understand it, Lambie. We're not mad at you.

HAUSER. *(To Susan.)* You're not condoning this?

SUSAN. I'm certainly not condemning him before I've heard him. What did he do?

HAUSER. The man said nothing to him and Jay hit him in the face.

SUSAN. It just wasn't any "man." He provoked you in some way, didn't he, Jay?

HAUSER. How?

JAY. He didn't have to do anything. I know what kind of person he is.

HAUSER. *(To Susan.)* There you are.

SUSAN. All right, Jay. I understand. It's all right.

HAUSER. It is not all right! He assaulted somebody!

SUSAN. It wasn't "somebody," don't you understand? He didn't walk up to a man on the street and hit him for no reason.

HAUSER. Is it better to hit somebody you know? A neighbor? A friend?

JAY. He's not a friend.

SUSAN. He's not a friend to anybody in this house. We know Jack for what he is. If he comes around here, he's asking for trouble.

JAY. And he *got* it.

HAUSER. You'll have to apologize.

JAY. I'm not going to apologize! I didn't do anything wrong!

HAUSER. You hit a man. In the face. That's very wrong. You will apologize.

JAY. I won't.

HAUSER. You will if I tell you to.

JAY. Whose side are you on!?

SUSAN. You won't do it again, will you, Jay?

JAY. I won't have to.

SUSAN. Go on to your room now.

HAUSER. This is not something you can excuse him for, Sue. He has to be responsible for it.

SUSAN. I'm sure he's sorry. Say you're sorry, Jay.

HAUSER. That isn't good enough.

SUSAN. It's good enough for me! What do you owe that — person — Dan? How much do you expect me to put up with!

JAY. Who cares about him? *(Pause.)*

HAUSER. Nobody. Nobody in the whole world cares about him, and that's why you're going to apologize.

JAY. I'm not!

HAUSER. Come on, Jay. I'll go over there with you.

JAY. No.

SUSAN. Leave him alone, Dan. He doesn't have to do this!

HAUSER. He does, while he's under my roof. He'll behave with decency as long as he is in my house.

SUSAN. It's my house, too! *(Hauser grabs Jay's wrist. Jay jerks away.)*

HAUSER. Come with me, Jay.

SUSAN. Dan. *(Pause.)* Why does he mean so much to you? Why don't you hate him, too?

JAY. Jesus, after what he did to you!

HAUSER. What he did ... Jay, go to your room.

JAY. What are you going to do?

HAUSER. Go to your room, goddamnit! Do what I tell you! *(Stunned by the language from his father, Jay exits.)*

SUSAN. What is he to you, Dan?

HAUSER. He's a human being, isn't that enough? ... Don't we have enough compassion to cover this, Sue? Is his offense so great? That's how he is.

SUSAN. You're very forgiving, very understanding all of a sudden. You've sent men to jail for being that way.

HAUSER. No. For what they *did*. Not for what they were.

SUSAN. Is there a difference?

HAUSER. Jay hit him just because he doesn't approve of him.

SUSAN. Jay hit him for what he did. What he did to *you*, Dan. Shouldn't Jack be punished for forcing himself on you?

HAUSER. We've abolished public flogging.

SUSAN. Don't you want him punished? You're willing to drag your own son over there to apologize. How about an apology from Jack? How about that much at least? *(Pause.)* He owes you one, doesn't he?

HAUSER. He's punished every day. Can't we leave him alone?

SUSAN. Doesn't he owe you even an apology, Dan? He did force himself on you. *(Pause.)* Didn't he?

HAUSER. He didn't have a weapon, if that's what you mean.

SUSAN. Just a simple answer, Dan. Did he force himself on you or not?

HAUSER. It wasn't that simple.

SUSAN. Did he force you?

HAUSER. Well … Can't we drop this? Isn't it over?

SUSAN. How long had you known he was that way? *(Pause.)*

HAUSER. I just want Jay to behave properly.

SUSAN. Did you know before you allowed me to start entertaining him? Did you know who I had in my house?

HAUSER. The man is *human.*

SUSAN. Suppose you let me decide that.

HAUSER. You don't "decide" …

SUSAN. How long did you know!

HAUSER. Jay must be taught that no matter …

SUSAN. This is not about Jay! Did you know what kind of person he was before you sat down and drank with him? *(Pause.)* I think I deserve an answer.

HAUSER. This is beside the point, Jay …

SUSAN. I think eighteen years of marriage entitles me to an honest answer.

HAUSER. I am always honest with you.

SUSAN. Are you? I always thought so, but maybe I've been naïve. You're not a saint, Daniel. You're rather alarmingly good sometimes, but you're not a saint.

HAUSER. I never claimed to be.

SUSAN. So give me an honest answer. How long had you known?

HAUSER. Why are you pressing this?

SUSAN. You haven't told me what it was like with him … Was it good?

HAUSER. Susan, for God's sake!

SUSAN. Oh, it disgusts you *now,* is that it?

HAUSER. We've been through all this …

SUSAN. No, we haven't. We've avoided all this. Did you think I'd forgotten it? Did you think I didn't have a thousand questions? Just answer me one. Did you know about Jack before he started dancing with you?

HAUSER. When does it stop?

SUSAN. If you honor the time we've spent together, tell me the truth. *(Pause.)*

HAUSER. I'd known for years.

SUSAN. I see.

HAUSER. I knew when he came over.

SUSAN. *(To stop him.)* All right.

HAUSER. I knew when he asked me to dance.

SUSAN. *(Trying to laugh.)* I didn't want a full confession.

HAUSER. You had to know. You had to know.

SUSAN. Oh, God, Dan. Why didn't you have sense enough to lie?

HAUSER. Because all the lying has exhausted me.

SUSAN. Oh, don't tell me that. Don't tell me that.

HAUSER. You insist on knowing.

SUSAN. I don't. I don't ... Didn't you ever love me?

HAUSER. Good God, Susan, I've always loved you. You're the best friend I've ever had. I married you because I couldn't bear to be without you. I wasn't a high school boy looking for sex. I was an adult looking for a friend for a lifetime. I chose to spend my life with *you. (Jay enters, unseen, listening.)*

SUSAN. But you wanted that. All the time you wanted someone like Jack. *(Pause.)*

HAUSER. I didn't do it. I didn't act on it. I wanted to be *normal.* I lived a normal life.

SUSAN. But you wanted it.

HAUSER. I couldn't help what I wanted! I could only control what I did! How can I make you understand?

SUSAN. I don't want to understand, keep it to yourself. *(Hauser notices Jay for the first time.)* Oh, Jay. *(Jay turns and exits.)*

HAUSER. Son ... *(Hauser and Susan exit after Jay. Jason enters.)*

JASON. There are some wounds for which the only balm is forgiveness, a medicine in ever short supply, made in the human heart and most needed when it is hardest to come by. My mother and I were schooled in making judgments, not acceptance, and if to understand is to forgive, what chance had we? We knew so little. We all knew so little. *(Morning. The scene is the same as the opening moment of the play. Hauser enters for breakfast. His heartiness is forced now.)*

HAUSER. *(Singing.)* "Bringing in the sheaves, bringing in the sheaves ... we shall come rejoicing, bringing in the sheaves ... " *(Susan enters to serve him. She is dressed for her job, looks sharper than previously.)* Good morning, my love. How are you this morning? *(He takes her hand, which she allows him to hold for a moment before withdrawing it.)*

SUSAN. I'm fine. *(Pause.)*

HAUSER. Jay! Up and at 'em! Rise and shine! *(Jay enters, slouching, shirt untucked, sullen. Cheerily.)* There he is, leader of tomorrow. Hard to believe, isn't it? *(Jay slumps into his chair.)*

JAY. *(Mumbled.)* Morning.

HAUSER. Hard to believe ... sit up straight, son. *(Jay does not change his posture.)* So ... what's on everyone's agenda for today?

SUSAN. I'll be working till late today, I believe. You'll have to fix something for Jay and yourself.

HAUSER. I guess we can manage that together, can't we Jay?

JAY. I guess ... gotta go.

HAUSER. Be at my office by noon, all right, Jay?

JAY. What for?

HAUSER. It's the father-and-son luncheon, I told you last week.

JAY. I'm not going to that.

HAUSER. We go every year.

JAY. I'm not going this year.

HAUSER. Of course you are. I look forward to showing you off.

SUSAN. Jay, you can do this. It means a lot to him.

HAUSER. Don't plead with him, Susan. I'm not asking anything all that difficult. It's the members of the Lion's Club and their sons. You're my son, you'll be there. *(Pause. Jay says nothing.)*

SUSAN. Say yes, it won't hurt you.

JAY. That's easy for you to say, Mom. You don't have to be seen with him.

SUSAN. Jay!

HAUSER. What?!

JAY. Do you expect me to stand up there with him in the middle of a room full of men? Everybody looking at us, everybody thinking.

HAUSER. Thinking what?

JAY. You know what.

HAUSER. Thinking what?

SUSAN. Jay, no one is thinking anything.

JAY. Oh, aren't they?!

SUSAN. Jay, they can't know. How would they know?

JAY. They can tell just by looking at him. You can see it in the way he moves, the way he holds his hands, the way he talks! What difference does it make how they know? It's true, isn't it? Isn't it? *(Susan turns away unable to answer. To Hauser.)* Isn't it? Isn't it true?! Isn't it! *(Pause.)*

HAUSER. Jay ...

JAY. Isn't it!

SUSAN. For God's sake, Dan, tell him it isn't true ... No, Jay, it's not true. He had too much to drink, they were ... they were wrestling, they fell on the bed ...

HAUSER. Sue, don't.

SUSAN. Then you tell him! Tell him what he has to hear.

HAUSER. Jay, I'm your father. I have loved you all of your life. I've done everything I knew how to do to prepare you for the world, I've given you everything I had to give. Is there nothing about me you can be proud of?

JASON. Practically everything.

JAY. No.

HAUSER. Nothing that would let you stand by my side in public and say, this is my father?

JAY. No!

HAUSER. *(Crushed.)* Oh, son. You were my triumph. My great accomplishment.

SUSAN. Dan, just tell him no! Just tell him!

HAUSER. I cannot live this way. I will not live this way.

SUSAN. Then tell him what he has to hear!

HAUSER. I want him to be proud of *me* … I want him to acknowledge me.

SUSAN. He can't. No one can.

HAUSER. I can't force you to accept me — but I won't live with your contempt.

JAY. You ought to be in jail. It's against the law, isn't it? Isn't it, Dad? Don't people go to jail for stuff like that?

SUSAN. You don't mean that! He's your father!

JAY. He's not my father. Queers can't be fathers. *(Directly to Hauser.)* Why don't you arrest yourself?

HAUSER. I'm not that brave, son, but I will do what I can for you. *(Hauser exits.)*

SUSAN. How could you be so cruel?

JAY. Me? What did I do? *(Susan exits. Jay is left alone. Despite his efforts, the awareness of his cruelty begins to hit him. Plaintively.)* Dad? … I didn't mean that …

JASON. *(Urgently.)* Then go and tell him! … Go! … Go! … *(Jay takes a step toward his father's direction, but ultimately his pride won't let him.)*

JAY. He made me say it. *(Jay exits in other direction.)*

JASON. He didn't make me say it — but why did he let me? … There were no more songs at the breakfast table after that. In six weeks he had resigned, put his affairs in order, and was gone to New York. My mother converted her part-time work at the radio station to a successful career that ultimately took her to Omaha, and then Chicago. But he was gone, and with him his world of order tempered by compassion. A temporary fiction, sustained by his will. He sent a monthly check, and with it a letter to me, usually brief, with little news but full of honest urgings for my success in life, my formation as an honorable man. Reading between the lines, I learned that he found a place for himself in the city, a niche where he felt comfortable at last with *all* of himself. He lived quietly for several years with a new friend, peacefully, happy, I think. But no longer in my world. He died before I was thirty of a heart that simply gave out. He died before the tide of history and my own maturation could teach me understanding ... before I was worthy of his forgiveness ... And now I raise my own son, Danny, in a time and place very different from Cascade, trying to prepare him for an altered universe. I talk to him about decency and compassion and tolerance — and I hear the echo of my father's voice in every word I speak. He listens with half an ear.

End of Play

PROPERTY LIST

Coffee
Briefcase with papers (HAUSER, JAY)
Bowl of cereal (SUSAN)
Mirror (SUSAN)
Flower (JACK)
Tray of food (SUSAN)
Bourbon, glasses (HAUSER)
Book (JACK)
Books (JAY)
Plates, tableware (SUSAN)
Pancakes (SUSAN)
Platter (SUSAN)

NEW PLAYS

★ **MONTHS ON END by Craig Pospisil.** In comic scenes, one for each month of the year, we follow the intertwined worlds of a circle of friends and family whose lives are poised between happiness and heartbreak. "…a triumph…these twelve vignettes all form crucial pieces in the eternal puzzle known as human relationships, an area in which the playwright displays an assured knowledge that spans deep sorrow to unbounded happiness." *—Ann Arbor News.* "…rings with emotional truth, humor…[an] endearing contemplation on love…entertaining and satisfying." *—Oakland Press.* [5M, 5W] ISBN: 0-8222-1892-5

★ **GOOD THING by Jessica Goldberg.** Brings us into the households of John and Nancy Roy, forty-something high-school guidance counselors whose marriage has been increasingly on the rocks and Dean and Mary, recent graduates struggling to make their way in life. "…a blend of gritty social drama, poetic humor and unsubtle existential contemplation…" *—Variety.* [3M, 3W] ISBN: 0-8222-1869-0

★ **THE DEAD EYE BOY by Angus MacLachlan.** Having fallen in love at their Narcotics Anonymous meeting, Billy and Shirley-Diane are striving to overcome the past together. But their relationship is complicated by the presence of Sorin, Shirley-Diane's fourteen-year-old son, a damaged reminder of her dark past. "…a grim, insightful portrait of an unmoored family…" *—NY Times.* "MacLachlan's play isn't for the squeamish, but then, tragic stories delivered at such an unrelenting fever pitch rarely are." *—Variety.* [1M, 1W, 1 boy] ISBN: 0-8222-1844-5

★ **[SIC] by Melissa James Gibson.** In adjacent apartments three young, ambitious neighbors come together to discuss, flirt, argue, share their dreams and plan their futures with unequal degrees of deep hopefulness and abject despair. "A work…concerned with the sound and power of language…" *—NY Times.* "…a wonderfully original take on urban friendship and the comedy of manners—a *Design for Living* for our times…" *—NY Observer.* [3M, 2W] ISBN: 0-8222-1872-0

★ **LOOKING FOR NORMAL by Jane Anderson.** Roy and Irma's twenty-five-year marriage is thrown into turmoil when Roy confesses that he is actually a woman trapped in a man's body, forcing the couple to wrestle with the meaning of their marriage and the delicate dynamics of family. "Jane Anderson's bittersweet transgender domestic comedy-drama …is thoughtful and touching and full of wit and wisdom. A real audience pleaser." *—Hollywood Reporter.* [5M, 4W] ISBN: 0-8222-1857-7

★ **ENDPAPERS by Thomas McCormack.** The regal Joshua Maynard, the old and ailing head of a mid-sized, family-owned book-publishing house in New York City, must name a successor. One faction in the house backs a smart, "pragmatic" manager, the other faction a smart, "sensitive" editor and both factions fear what the other's man could do to this house— and to them. "If Kaufman and Hart had undertaken a comedy about the publishing business, they might have written *Endpapers*…a breathlessly fast, funny, and thoughtful comedy …keeps you amused, guessing, and often surprised…profound in its empathy for the paradoxes of human nature." *—NY Magazine.* [7M, 4W] ISBN: 0-8222-1908-5

★ **THE PAVILION by Craig Wright.** By turns poetic and comic, romantic and philosophical, this play asks old lovers to face the consequences of difficult choices made long ago. "The script's greatest strength lies in the genuineness of its feeling." *—Houston Chronicle.* "Wright's perceptive, gently witty writing makes this familiar situation fresh and thoroughly involving." *—Philadelphia Inquirer.* [2M, 1W (flexible casting)] ISBN: 0-8222-1898-4

DRAMATISTS PLAY SERVICE, INC.
440 Park Avenue South, New York, NY 10016 212-683-8960 Fax 212-213-1539
postmaster@dramatists.com www.dramatists.com

NEW PLAYS

★ **BE AGGRESSIVE by Annie Weisman.** Vista Del Sol is paradise, sandy beaches, avocado-lined streets. But for seventeen-year-old cheerleader Laura, everything changes when her mother is killed in a car crash, and she embarks on a journey to the Spirit Institute of the South where she can learn "cheer" with Bible belt intensity. "…filled with lingual gymnastics…stylized rapid-fire dialogue…" *–Variety.* "…a new, exciting, and unique voice in the American theatre…" *–BackStage West.* [1M, 4W, extras] ISBN: 0-8222-1894-1

★ **FOUR by Christopher Shinn.** Four people struggle desperately to connect in this quiet, sophisticated, moving drama. "…smart, broken-hearted…Mr. Shinn has a precocious and forgiving sense of how power shifts in the game of sexual pursuit…He promises to be a playwright to reckon with…" *–NY Times.* "A voice emerges from an American place. It's got humor, sadness and a fresh and touching rhythm that tell of the loneliness and secrets of life…[a] poetic, haunting play." *–NY Post.* [3M, 1W] ISBN: 0-8222-1850-X

★ **WONDER OF THE WORLD by David Lindsay-Abaire.** A madcap picaresque involving Niagara Falls, a lonely tour-boat captain, a pair of bickering private detectives and a husband's dirty little secret. "Exceedingly whimsical and playfully wicked. Winning and genial. A top-drawer production." *–NY Times.* "Full frontal lunacy is on display. A most assuredly fresh and hilarious tragicomedy of marital discord run amok…absolutely hysterical…" *–Variety.* [3M, 4W (doubling)] ISBN: 0-8222-1863-1

★ **QED by Peter Parnell.** Nobel Prize-winning physicist and all-around genius Richard Feynman holds forth with captivating wit and wisdom in this fascinating biographical play that originally starred Alan Alda. "QED is a seductive mix of science, human affections, moral courage, and comic eccentricity. It reflects on, among other things, death, the absence of God, travel to an unexplored country, the pleasures of drumming, and the need to know and understand." *–NY Magazine.* "Its rhythms correspond to the way that people—even geniuses—approach and avoid highly emotional issues, and it portrays Feynman with affection and awe." *–The New Yorker.* [1M, 1W] ISBN: 0-8222-1924-7

★ **UNWRAP YOUR CANDY by Doug Wright.** Alternately chilling and hilarious, this deliciously macabre collection of four bedtime tales for adults is guaranteed to keep you awake for nights on end. "Engaging and intellectually satisfying…a treat to watch." *–NY Times.* "Fiendishly clever. Mordantly funny and chilling. Doug Wright teases, freezes and zaps us." *–Village Voice.* "Four bite-size plays that bite back." *–Variety.* [flexible casting] ISBN: 0-8222-1871-2

★ **FURTHER THAN THE FURTHEST THING by Zinnie Harris.** On a remote island in the middle of the Atlantic secrets are buried. When the outside world comes calling, the islanders find their world blown apart from the inside as well as beyond. "Harris winningly produces an intimate and poetic, as well as political, family saga." *–Independent (London).* "Harris' enthralling adventure of a play marks a departure from stale, well-furrowed theatrical terrain." *–Evening Standard (London).* [3M, 2W] ISBN: 0-8222-1874-7

★ **THE DESIGNATED MOURNER by Wallace Shawn.** The story of three people living in a country where what sort of books people like to read and how they choose to amuse themselves becomes both firmly personal and unexpectedly entangled with questions of survival. "This is a playwright who does not just tell you what it is like to be arrested at night by goons or to fall morally apart and become an aimless yet weirdly contented ghost yourself. He has the originality to make you feel it." *–Times (London).* "A fascinating play with beautiful passages of writing…" *–Variety.* [2M, 1W] ISBN: 0-8222-1848-8

DRAMATISTS PLAY SERVICE, INC.
440 Park Avenue South, New York, NY 10016 212-683-8960 Fax 212-213-1539
postmaster@dramatists.com www.dramatists.com

NEW PLAYS

★ **SHEL'S SHORTS by Shel Silverstein.** Lauded poet, songwriter and author of children's books, the incomparable Shel Silverstein's short plays are deeply infused with the same wicked sense of humor that made him famous. "…[a] childlike honesty and twisted sense of humor." *–Boston Herald.* "…terse dialogue and an absurdity laced with a tang of dread give [*Shel's Shorts*] more than a trace of Samuel Beckett's comic existentialism." *–Boston Phoenix.* [flexible casting] ISBN: 0-8222-1897-6

★ **AN ADULT EVENING OF SHEL SILVERSTEIN by Shel Silverstein.** Welcome to the darkly comic world of Shel Silverstein, a world where nothing is as it seems and where the most innocent conversation can turn menacing in an instant. These ten imaginative plays vary widely in content, but the style is unmistakable. "…[*An Adult Evening*] shows off Silverstein's virtuosic gift for wordplay…[and] sends the audience out…with a clear appreciation of human nature as perverse and laughable." *–NY Times.* [flexible casting] ISBN: 0-8222-1873-9

★ **WHERE'S MY MONEY? by John Patrick Shanley.** A caustic and sardonic vivisection of the institution of marriage, laced with the author's inimitable razor-sharp wit. "…Shanley's gift for acid-laced one-liners and emotionally tumescent exchanges is certainly potent…" *–Variety.* "…lively, smart, occasionally scary and rich in reverse wisdom." *–NY Times.* [3M, 3W] ISBN: 0-8222-1865-8

★ **A FEW STOUT INDIVIDUALS by John Guare.** A wonderfully screwy comedy-drama that figures Ulysses S. Grant in the throes of writing his memoirs, surrounded by a cast of fantastical characters, including the Emperor and Empress of Japan, the opera star Adelina Patti and Mark Twain. "Guare's smarts, passion and creativity skyrocket to awesome heights…" *–Star Ledger.* "…precisely the kind of good new play that you might call an everyday miracle…every minute of it is fresh and newly alive…" *–Village Voice.* [10M, 3W] ISBN: 0-8222-1907-7

★ **BREATH, BOOM by Kia Corthron.** A look at fourteen years in the life of Prix, a Bronx native, from her ruthless girl-gang leadership at sixteen through her coming to maturity at thirty. "…vivid world, believable and eye-opening, a place worthy of a dramatic visit, where no one would want to live but many have to." *–NY Times.* "…rich with humor, terse vernacular strength and gritty detail…" *–Variety.* [1M, 9W] ISBN: 0-8222-1849-6

★ **THE LATE HENRY MOSS by Sam Shepard.** Two antagonistic brothers, Ray and Earl, are brought together after their father, Henry Moss, is found dead in his seedy New Mexico home in this classic Shepard tale. "…His singular gift has been for building mysteries out of the ordinary ingredients of American family life…" *–NY Times.* "…rich moments …Shepard finds gold." *–LA Times.* [7M, 1W] ISBN: 0-8222-1858-5

★ **THE CARPETBAGGER'S CHILDREN by Horton Foote.** One family's history spanning from the Civil War to WWII is recounted [...] monologues. "…bittersweet music—[a] rhapsody [...] way…theatrically daring." *–The New Yorker.* [3W [...]

★ **THE NINA VARIATIONS by Steven Diet[...]** homage to *The Seagull*, Dietz puts Chekhov's sta[...] them out. "A perfect little jewel of a play…" *–She[...]* elation of a writer at play; and also an odd, hau[...] beauty." *–Eastside Journal (Seattle).* [1M, 1W (fle[...]

DRAMATISTS PLAY [...]
440 Park Avenue South, New York, NY 1001[...]
postmaster@dramatists.com